Delaware

The high-profile Delaware Memorial Bridge Twin Span
cables the First State to New Jersey over the Delaware River.

Ruth Ann Minner

photographs by
Kevin Fleming

text by Nancy E. Lynch

ISBN 0-9662423-5-1 • copyright ©MMI by Kevin Fleming • all rights reserved

Diversity defines New Castle County, from rolling hills studded with extravagant estates to cityscapes to muskrat marshes edging busy waterways. Smallest of Delaware's three counties at 437 square miles, New Castle County wraps wetlands, parks and fertile farmland around Wilmington, Delaware's largest city and America's corporate capital. Its 17th century roots were sown by Swedish, Dutch and English immigrants who settled on the banks of the Christina and Delaware rivers. Today, more than 500,000 people call the county home.

Industry dawned early in Wilmington. Settled as New Sweden in 1638, Wilmington became one of the mid-Atlantic's most important 19th century industrial sites with the manufacture of black powder on Brandywine Creek. The DuPont Company's evolution to the country's largest chemical and materials conglomerate showered prosperity on the city and opened doors for other businesses. Today, numerous manufacturing and financial institutions broaden Wilmington's busy skyline. Favorable incorporation laws attract nearly 60 percent of Fortune 500 companies and Delaware has more Ph.D.s per capita than any other state.

New Jersey shore to port, a waterman (left) checks his crab pots at sunrise on the Delaware River in southern New Castle County. "You can't take your pots out and let them sit – you have to tend them every 72 hours by law," explains commercial crabber Steve Pyle of Odessa. Territorial rights are up for grabs. "It's first come, first served. If you go out and no one's there, you can start laying your lines. Basically, everyone tries to get along," he says of the state's 200 or so licensed crabbers. "You work sunup to sundown, seven days a week but once you've done it you can't give it up."

"I saw this barn and had to have it," Sal De Paulo says of the 19th century stucco, fieldstone and frame outbuilding mirrored in Maple Brook Farm's spring-fed pond near Centreville (following pages). "It was in pretty bad shape when we bought it in 1985. We nailed siding and put a new cedar shake roof on it. Amish from Pennsylvania paint it every five years. Everybody likes it." De Paulo decorates his much-photographed barn on the Kennett Pike with a 14-foot diameter wreath at Christmas and a 20-by-40-foot American flag on Independence Day. The pegged-beam barn is dated 1844 and signed by Benjamin Walker Recktor and John Barton Clark, who inscribed "Learn of me, be humble in these latter days" on its north interior wall. "I'd heard about this barn before we bought it," adds De Paulo's wife, Gerrie. "People take pictures constantly. I'm barned to death."

Serendipity rains on Aaron E. Honie (following pages) of Wilmington, son Aaron T. and friend Leondrei Salters-Simmins as they relax in Brandywine Creek. "I live a couple of blocks away on West Street and try to get here every day." Honie swims and fishes above the waterfall, walks his three dogs, bikes and picnics in the park near Brandywine Zoo and Monkey Hill.

Gridlock of great import, foreign-made cars checker the Port of Wilmington (right) which posted its busiest year in 2000 with a record 5 million short tons of cargo. A bid to bring Toyota Motor Corporation's Northeastern seaboard auto shipping operations to Wilmington would jump-start the port, already handling Volkswagen imports. "In 2001, we anticipate a nice increase," says port marketing manager Vered Nohi-Becker. Established in 1923 and owned and operated by Diamond State Port Corporation, the facility leads the nation in beef imports and dominates as the East Coast gateway for worldwide fruit and produce imports. More foreign bananas and apple, pear and orange juice concentrates flow through Wilmington's docks than any others nationwide. Vital to Wilmington's economy, the port employs 5,800 workers and pays $22 million in state and local taxes. A $28 million auto berth, open in 2002, drives ambitious expansion along the Delaware River near the port's single 4,000-foot pier on the Christina River.

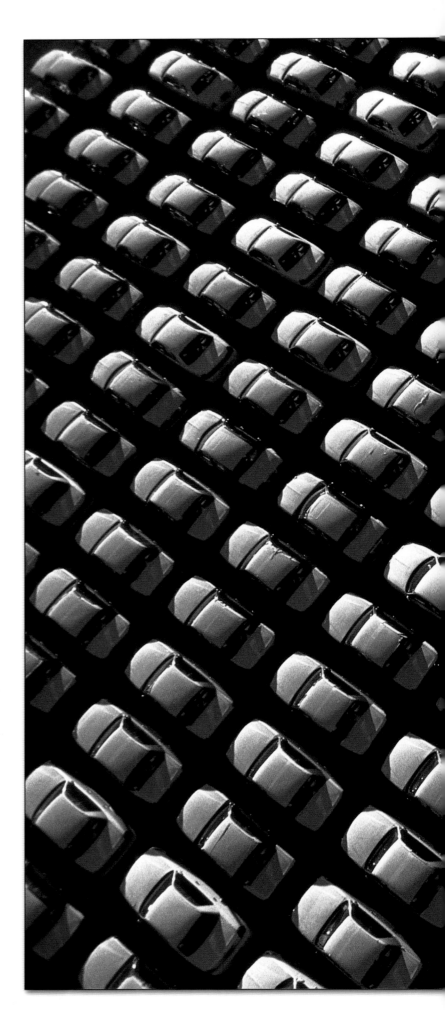

"Nobody really wants to be a longshoreman today, it's a dying trade," says second-generation Port of Wilmington worker John Uryc (above). "The freedom of coming to work or not coming to work is the good part. But if the big fish are running, I just might go fishing."

Out of this world, the Saturn L-Series (following pages) sent buyers into orbit when the mid-size car debuted nationally in July 1999 as an alternative to the smaller S-Series Saturn. "The initial response was extremely positive," recalls Saturn Corporation spokeswoman Alice Petitt at the Wilmington Assembly Plant on Boxwood Road, the company's only L-Series production site. "However, due to recent declines in market demand, the plant was forced to reduce its production in June, 2000 to a one-shift operation with 2,100 employees and a projected volume of 104,000 vehicles this year. It's all economics."

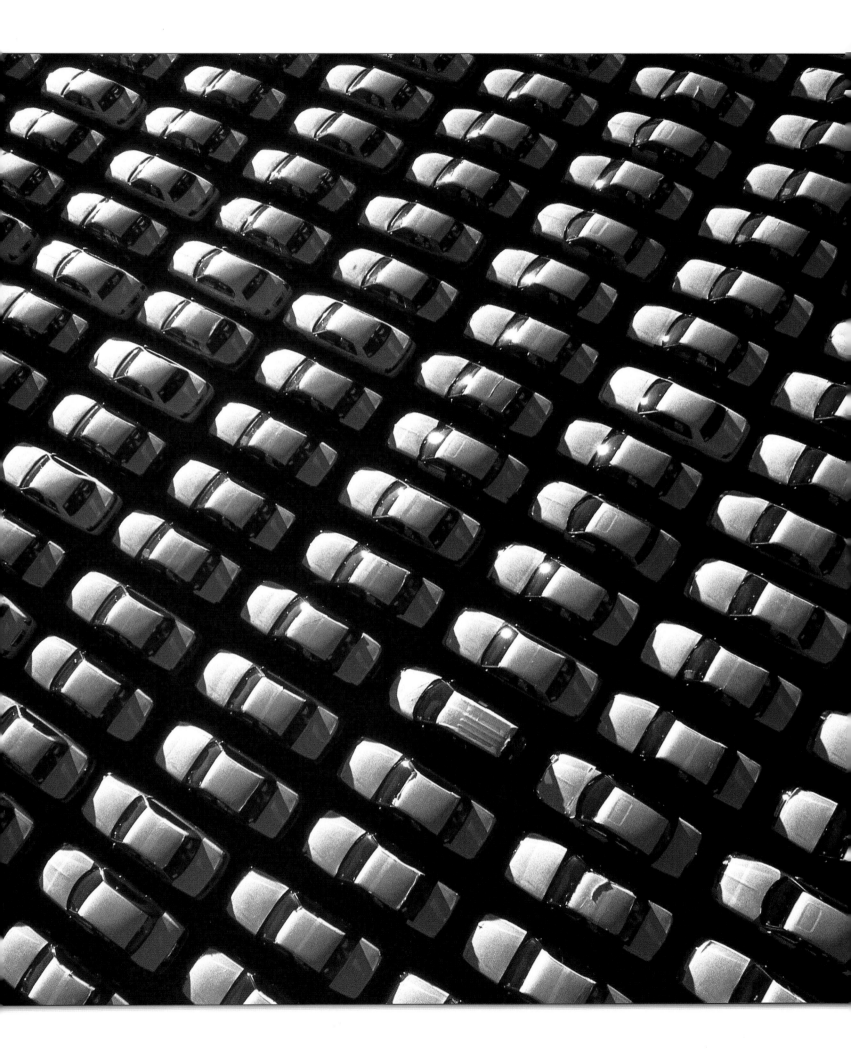

Having a ball, Dan Johnson swings into action while twin brother Reid plots his next move and neighbor Casey Englebert readies for the rebound (right). "That ball's the best investment I ever made in summer entertainment. My kids play with it every day," the twins' mom, Kim Johnson, says of the oversized vinyl orb in the family's Delaware Avenue back yard. "They kick it, they jump on it. Kids in the neighborhood love it. So do their parents, as long as I keep it in my yard. My husband thought I was crazy because I spent about $100 on this ball. I told him the kids were going to love it. I was right."

"Wilmington's a great city. It's growing and there are a lot of advantages to living here that encourage families to get together," says lifelong resident Melissa Ewell. Summer in the city means outdoor fun for Fourth Street resident Ikea Dickerson (above). "I like to jump around and sometimes I practice jump roping," the E.G. Shortlidge Elementary School student says as her mother, Letitia, and brother, Kendell, work the rope for her. "I like it when the sun's coming out so I can be outside and play with my friends."

"The Blue Danube Ball is the best-kept secret in Delaware," Ruth Babiy says of the elegant fund-raiser in the Hotel du Pont's Gold Ballroom (right) where about 200 gather annually to enjoy Austrian culture. Sumptuous Viennese fare precedes artistic interludes and traditional dances at the black-tie affair sponsored by the Austrian-American Society of Delaware. "You don't have to know how to dance the Polonaise. Everybody takes a partner and it's basically a three-step. Everyone loves to do it," says Babiy, perennial co-chair of the event organized in 1969 by former WDEL radio personality Charlotte Shedd and Adele Weaver.

Corps de ballet members from the Wilmington Ballet Company (following pages), the city's first resident professional ballet company, fidget in the hotel's marble foyer awaiting their cue to perform. Under the direction of Victor Wesley, ballerinas dance to music in keeping with the ball's Austrian theme. The evening's proceeds provide a $7,000 scholarship to a promising young Delaware musician or singer, chosen through audition at the Wilmington Music School, for six weeks of summer study at the Mozarteum in Salzburg, Austria. New Castle-born Kathleen Cassello, one of the Three Sopranos, earned the 1984 stipend. Each scholarship winner must perform at the Blue Danube Ball "so those attending," Babiy says, "can see what they're sponsoring."

Centerpiece of Chateau Country, Granogue (right) dominates northern New Castle County's rolling hills as a weather-proof reminder of the influence and frequent indulgence of the duPont family in Delaware. Built of Germantown granite over 18 months and completed in 1923 by Irénée duPont, president of the DuPont Company from 1919 to 1926, the 11-bedroom mansion is 362 feet above sea level. Granogue was home to duPont, his wife, Irene, and their eight daughters and a son. For nearly 30 years, it served as backdrop for duPont's lavish Fourth of July fireworks parties. "The structure itself will stand the ages," says

current resident Irénée duPont Jr. "It's going to be the devil's own job to tear it down but not on my watch. I look at it as a tool for carrying on the thoughts and philosophy from one generation to another. I have the highest esteem for my parents for giving me that privilege."

A water tower, also of Germantown granite, (above) stands sentry on the 515-acre estate.

Turf's up for thoroughbred and Arabian racing April through November at Delaware Park in Stanton (preceding pages). Designed by William duPont Jr. and opened in 1937 as the East Coast's only major track outside Aqueduct for June racing, the verdant 600-acre venue hosts the $600,000 Delaware Handicap each July. "We have a reputation for being one of the prettiest tracks around. Our paddock and grove are signature pieces," says Delaware Park spokesman Chris Sobocinski. Leading jockey Mike Smith recently raced at Delaware Park for the first time. "There's a lot of history here. There's also a family atmosphere. You just walk in and see the beautiful saddling area, the big ol' trees. It reminds me a bit of Saratoga." When bettors tire of horses at Delaware's only thoroughbred track, they wager at 2,000 slot machines nearby. "The addition of slots in 1995 allows Delaware Park to increase purses," says Sobocinski. "That makes our product more attractive and lets us stay competitive, now that Baltimore and Pennsylvania have their own tracks."

Winterthur's annual Point-to-Point amateur steeplechase races (right) take off each May as one of Wilmington's social highlights with high fashion, antique carriages, corporate tents and tailgate picnics. "The event started out in 1979 as really something for horse people but it's grown to be so much more," says Winterthur spokeswoman Hillary K. Holland. The one-day fundraiser attracts crowds of 26,000 and has netted more than $3.5 million for Henry Francis duPont's acclaimed early American decorative arts museum and gardens north of Wilmington.

Even with 175 period rooms, Winterthur always dresses for the holidays, re-creating seasonal celebrations of the 18th and 19th centuries. The duPont Dining Room (right) and Montmorenci Staircase (below) deck the halls, bringing to life Lucy Ellen Merrill's circa 1870 drawing, "A Victorian Dining Room at Christmas," with Yuletide greens and

stacks of presents at each place. By adding a second flight to a circa 1822 circular staircase from North Carolina, Henry Francis duPont, who died in 1969, created an unusual elliptical shape. "We have something for everyone with rooms, galleries, gardens and a research library," Holland says. "And we're open 362 days a year so we can certainly keep you occupied."

"Growing poinsettias is a pain in the butt," says Michael Leubecker, manager of Floral Plant Growers near Middletown. "They're a long crop and they take a lot of effort." With greenhouses covering 10 acres, the business wholesales about 500,000 of the showy holiday flowers yearly to mass merchandisers primarily in Delaware, Maryland and Virginia. Worker Kaorn Caim (preceding pages) from Cambodia carries ready-for-market plants through a sea of Freedom Red poinsettias. "When you look at acres of red, white and pink, they are pretty," Leubecker allows. "But they're prettier when they're in someone's home and paid for."

Man of a million lights, Rich Faucher (left) illuminates the holidays for 60,000 visitors from five states. "I discovered the real meaning of Christmas years ago," says the father of six who makes Boeing aircraft parts in Ridley Park, Pennsylvania. "And there really is a Santa Claus. I try to keep that spirit alive." With nearly 80,000 strings of lights, he creates a different display each year. "When one display ends," he says, "the next one starts. It's Christmas 365 day a year here." Faucher recently doubled his 200-amp electrical service to accommodate the one-acre light show on Santa Claus Lane near Red Lion. "Every now and then, I sneak down the chimney, but Santa really enters through the heart."

"This is one of the few private residences in the state that gets a comment from historian J. Thomas Scharf, which tickles the hell out of me," Fritz Haase says of his 1877 Middletown home (following pages). The partially restored Second Empire Mansard-style structure, where Delaware Governor Benjamin Thomas Biggs died on Christmas Day, 1893, receives its annual floral flourish from Hasse's wife, Donna, and neighbor Laszlo Bodo.

31

Pretty as a picture, Laura Jogani (right) of Corner Ketch embraces her unusual family tree. "She and her younger sister, Elizabeth, are 50 percent Polish and 50 percent Indian," Suken Jogani says of his progeny. "My wife, Maria, is 100 percent Polish and I'm 100 percent Indian. Chances are they might be the only Polish-Indian kids in the state. It's not a very common mix." The couple met at the DuPont Company's Ag Products Division and recently returned to their Wilmington roots after a transfer to East Peoria, Illinois. "We're close to family, the neighborhood

has lots of kids and we like the rolling hills," says Jogani. "We like the ruralness of it even though it's not really rural."

Lost in his field of dreams, Tyler Warrington (above) of Hockessin watches a Delaware Semi-Pro League baseball game at Rockford Park. "He's a baseball fanatic. He eats, sleeps and drinks the game," says dad Alan, a Pike Creek family physician and head coach of HealthSouth, one of eight Delaware semi-pro teams. "Some nights he's a batboy and other nights he's just a big fan. He always like to have a catch with the players."

A larger-than-life St. Anthony (left) floats through Little Italy in an hour-long procession heralding the finale of the annual eight-day Italian Festival, Wilmington's first major ethnic celebration. Feeder of the poor, the patron saint of St. Anthony of Padua Roman Catholic Church symbolically oversees distribution of thousands of rolls along the route. The church on Wilmington's west side marked its 50th anniversary in 1975 by organizing the June festival. Today the event musters 600 volunteers and attracts 250,000 people who spend $1 million on food, rides, games and entertainment. Proceeds benefit church programs and St. Anthony's schools.

Fun comes in all flavors for Jenny Neuwien (above) as she nibbles on Joseph Sands at St. Hedwig's 43rd Polish Festival in Wilmington. "We were just having a good time," says Neuwien, whose family reunites at the city's oldest festival. "My dad, Nicky Neuwien, is a member of the church and he calls us every year. About 12 of us get together. It's nice to see everyone." The six-day festival's Polish food and polka bands always prove good habits for Felician Sisters Dorothy and Angela of Sacred Heart Convent. "It was the first time I'd been on a ride like that for 30 years," Sister Dorothy says of the Sizzler. "And it'll probably be another 30 years."

Completed in 1859 with granite walls up to 30 feet thick and massive firepower to protect the ports of Wilmington and Philadelphia, Fort Delaware on Pea Patch Island (right) in the Delaware River was the nation's largest and most advanced military fortification. Indoor flush toilets provided novel relief at the fort, constructed over 10 years at a cost of $2 million. During the Civil War, the pentagon-shaped Union fortress was converted to a prisoner-of-war camp and incarcerated nearly 13,000 Confederates after the Battle of Gettysburg. The fort, unique for its circular granite stairways and 30-foot moat, also was garrisoned during the Spanish-American War and both World Wars. No hostile shots ever were fired from Fort Delaware. Closed in 1944, the fortress was declared surplus federal property. Delaware acquired it three years later and turned it into one of its first state parks. Garrison Weekend, Fort Delaware's premier event, draws 300

East Coast interpreters like "prisoner" John Clarkson (above) of Shipman, Virginia, who bring 1864 to life every August.

To the north, Union re-enactors ponder battlefield strategy over coffee at Brandywine Creek State Park (following pages) where Civil War engagements are waged every Memorial Day weekend. "Battles start at 1 p.m. and last 45 minutes to an hour. Yanks win one and Confederates win one," seasonal park employee Jonathan Schneider says of the 1,500 East Coast re-enactors who occupy the park's 1,000 acres. "We're the only Delaware state park that does re-enacting. Even though no Civil War battles were ever fought here, it looks conceivable. There's something about them that transcends time."

River for all seasons, the rapid-flowing, rock-filled Brandywine (right) for centuries powered sawmills, grist, cotton, woolen, and paper mills as well as black powder manufacture along its banks. Early Lenni-Lenape inhabitants called the waterway Wawaset, meaning "near the bend." The Brandywine likely derives its name from Andren Brantwyn, one of Wilmington's first Swedish settlers. The creek, with headwaters in two branches that converge in Pennsylvania, flows more than 10 miles through northern New Castle County. It falls eight feet from the state line to Rockland Bridge – three-quarters of its length – then plummets 130 feet to its confluence with the Christina River. Now a recreational venue, the Brandywine supports canoeing, kayaking, tubing, rope-swinging, swimming, wading and picnicking.

Taking time for summer fun, Jenilee Delvalle (below) and her sister, Nidhya, of Wilmington relax with relatives on a Sunday afternoon near Smith's Bridge on the Brandywine River.

The first duPont family home, Eleutherian Mills (following pages) immortalizes an immigrant's success. French chemist and political refugee Eleuthere Irénée duPont in 1802 capitalized on water power from Brandywine Creek north of Wilmington to forge the nation's biggest gunpowder business. E.I Du Pont de Nemours and Company manufactured black powder at the original Hagley Mills until 1921. Subsequent diversification produced nylon, Dacron, Teflon, Lucite, Lycra and Kevlar, revolutionary inventions that propelled Du Pont to the industrial forefront as the country's largest chemical company. duPont's 1803 manse, on a hill overlooking the mills and home to five generations of duPonts, today is the centerpiece of the restored industrial community known as Hagley Museum.

"I'm part of a team that develops new materials, processes and applications for holograms," says physical chemist Sylvia Stevenson (right), working in a laser lab at the DuPont Company's Experimental Station. "Our business, DuPont Holographic Materials, produces a photopolymer film for recording holograms." Commercial applications include three-dimensional images used as security devices. "But our bigger market," adds Stevenson, a Californian with an Iowa State University doctorate, "is components that go into flat panel displays for devices like LCD watches, cell phones, pagers and laptop computers." One of the first research laboratories in the country, the Experimental Station opened in 1903 north of Wilmington on the original site of the employee country club. About 5,000 people, including 1,000 Ph.D.s, work at the 129-acre complex overlooking Brandywine Creek.

"You're looking at a schematic drawing of the molecule that is the active ingredient in a pill one can take for asthma," Dr. Fred Brown (above) says of Accolate, the prescription medicine he and his colleagues discovered about 14 years ago at Zeneca in Wilmington, long before his company's merger with Astra AB of Sweden. "We launched the drug in 1996 for U.S. consumption. Many asthma-sufferers have told us Accolate makes all the difference in their lives." The newly created AstraZeneca PLC, a $35 billion union of London-based Zeneca Group PLC and Astra, is one of the top five pharmaceutical companies in the world. The company is building its North American headquarters on 86 acres across from Zeneca's Fairfax campus.

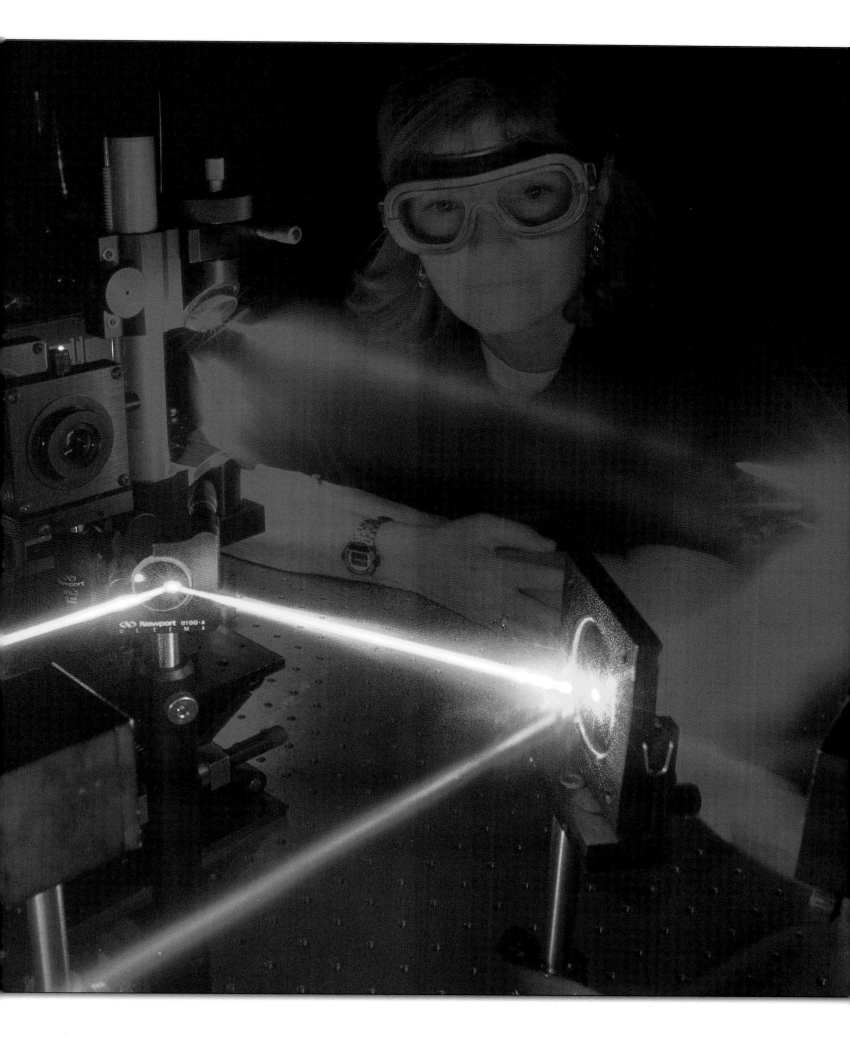

University of Delaware Blue Hen fullback James O'Neal (right) takes wing against Portland State University in an NCAA Division 1-AA playoff game. The Fightin' Blue Hens, named for the state's Revolutionary War troops who fought as fiercely as gamecocks, have five national championships under their helmets and were runners-up three other times. Legendary coach Tubby Raymond's 296 victories rank him ninth on the all-time collegiate coaching win list. New Ark College opened in 1834 as a degree-granting institution after the General Assembly established its perpetual charter. Renamed Delaware College in 1843, doors closed 16 years later for financial reasons and the

impending Civil War. The college reopened in 1870 under the federal Morrill Land Grant Act and state legislation in 1921 created the University of Delaware. More than 100,000 alumni live in 76 countries.

Tower Hill School field hockey players Kristen Diver and Alexandra Albright (above) thrill in their victory over Smyrna High School. "I expect them to give 100 percent on the field and just about always they do," says head coach Robin Adair. Tower Hillers won four consecutive state field hockey championships in the 1990s and players have gone on to compete on national teams and at the Junior Olympics.

"The sunrise was the perfect touch with
the water right there and the Delaware
Memorial Bridge in the background. It
was awsome," Judy Kiger (preceding
pages) says of the moment shared with
John Prater on New Castle's Delaware
Street wharf. Countless sunrises earlier,
William Penn first stepped on New World
soil near here. After the British conquest
of the Dutch in 1664, the town was granted
to Penn and named New Castle. "There's
a lot more in Delaware than where I live,"
says Kiger of Elsonboro, New Jersey. "I've
worked at restaurants in New Jersey but I
seem to do better in Delaware. I commute
daily and also come over to go to malls,
movies and to eat. I think about moving."

Crown jewel of the First State's first
capital, the 1732 New Castle Court House
(right) was the meeting place of the
Colonial Assembly and Delaware's first
General Assembly. The brick building
remained the State House until 1777 when
fears of attack by the British Navy
prompted establishment of an inland
capital in Dover. The cupola of the Court
House is the center of the 12-mile arc
separating Delaware from Pennsylvania.
Colonial Immanuel Church on The Green,
prominent with its 19th century tower and
steeple, is a foundation of the Episcopal
Church in Delaware. Founded as Fort
Casimir by the Dutch in 1651, New Castle
was the major port on the Delaware River
and home to Declaration of Independence
signers George Read, George Ross Jr. and
Thomas McKean.

Hoopes Reservoir (right) safeguards two billion gallons of water for the city of Wilmington and its New Castle County customers. Although spring-fed, most of the 30-day emergency water supply is diverted from Brandywine Creek. The 200-acre reservoir on property once owned by T. Coleman duPont is 130 feet at its deepest point and was built by the Wilmington Water Department on Old Mill Stream, a small tributary of Red Clay Creek northwest of the city. Flooding the area forever submerged duPont's summer home. The four-year project was completed in 1933 at a cost of $2.2 million and is named for the late Edgar M. Hoopes, a water department chief engineer. Along its conifer and hardwood perimeter posted signs forbid fishing, boating and swimming in the 50-degree

water. "It's an extraordinary natural asset. You couldn't build this reservoir today for love or money," says Delaware Department of Transportation Secretary Nathan Hayward III who lives nearby. "The fact the city was wise enough to prevent development along its shores is important. It was a far-sighted project."

"This class of rowers over four years was more successful than any other, male or female," coach Brad Bates says of his St. Andrew's School girls varsity eight team (above) led by stroke Meaghan Keeley of Clarksburg, West Virginia. Delaware's only secondary school crew teams practice and race on Noxontown Pond at the Middletown boarding school.

Rare beef, Belted Galloways (right) graze on Bayard Sharp's Centreville farm. Intrigued by the cow's unique look, Sharp bought his first Belties more than a decade ago and works diligently to improve his herd of about 50. Without the layer of backfat characteristic of most beef animals, this breed of Scottish lineage produces exceptionally lean and flavorful meat. Dressed weight exceeds 60 percent of live weight. Black Belties resemble Oreo cookies with their distinctive appearance, although the mid-size cows also sport red or dun coats sandwiching their signature white centers. Belted Galloways number about 6,000 nationally.

Brushed with a fall palette, artist Jamie Wyeth's farm (left) straddles Delaware and Pennsylvania where three generations of Wyeths have drawn inspiration from the area's fields, streams and rolling hills. Jamie, while hewing to the family trait of romantic realism and rural subjects, carved his own niche in the 1960s with portraits of President John F. Kennedy and the provocative leather-clad subject of "Draft Age." Born into the Brandywine school of painting through grandfather N.C. Wyeth, one of the nation's most prolific illustrators, and father Andrew Wyeth, one of America's favorite artists, Jamie tends toward N.C. in style and substance. The Delaware Art Museum in Wilmington and nearby Brandywine River Museum in Chadds Ford, Pennsylvania display many Wyeth works.

"We're doing something that's never happened before in

the history of painting. My students call it 'Loperism' until somebody finds a sensible name for it," says Wilmington artist Ed Loper (above). "I am an abstract colorist. I paint realistic pictures but I paint them with colors and abstract spaces." Spanning more than six decades, his work is inspired by French impressionist Paul Cézanne. Loper studied under the late Violette de Mazia at Pennsylvania's Barnes Foundation. "I went there to learn from her how to understand art. And I learned," says Loper. "Painting is not talent, it's a seeing process and you learn to see. I look at something and if I think it's worthwhile in terms of lines and spaces and color, then I paint it. It's that simple."

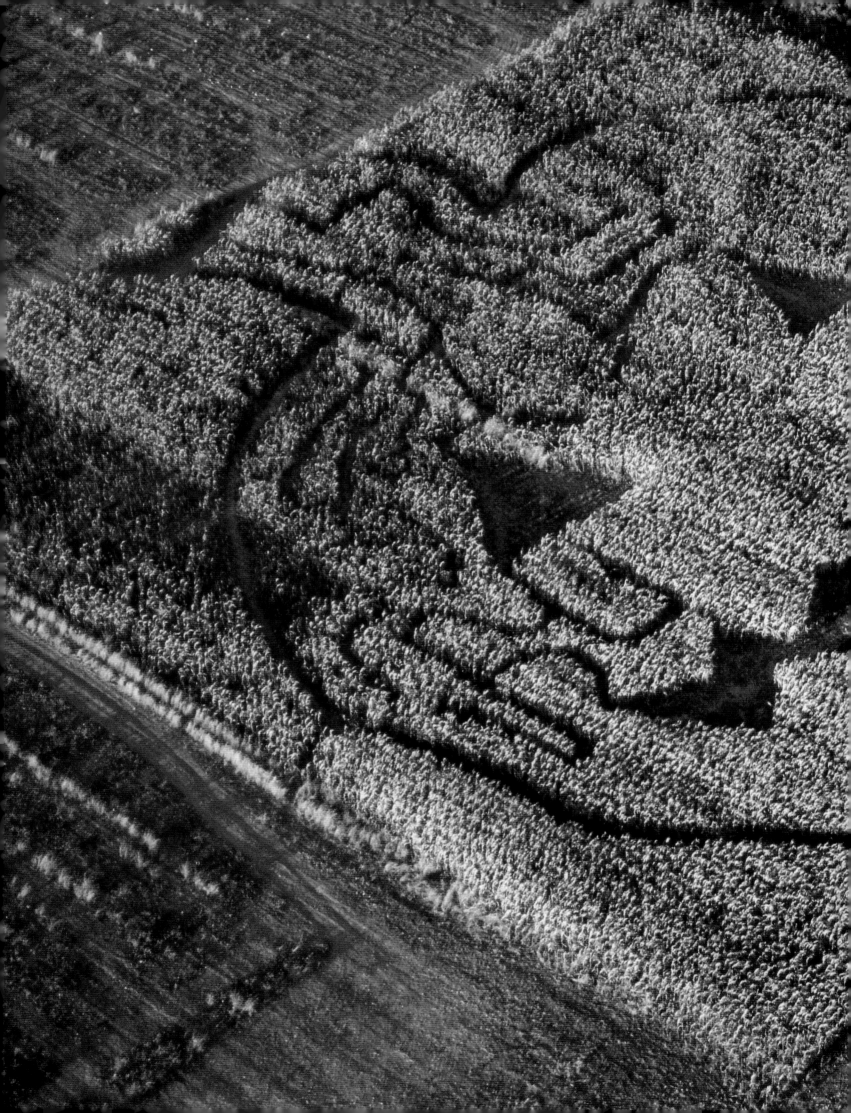

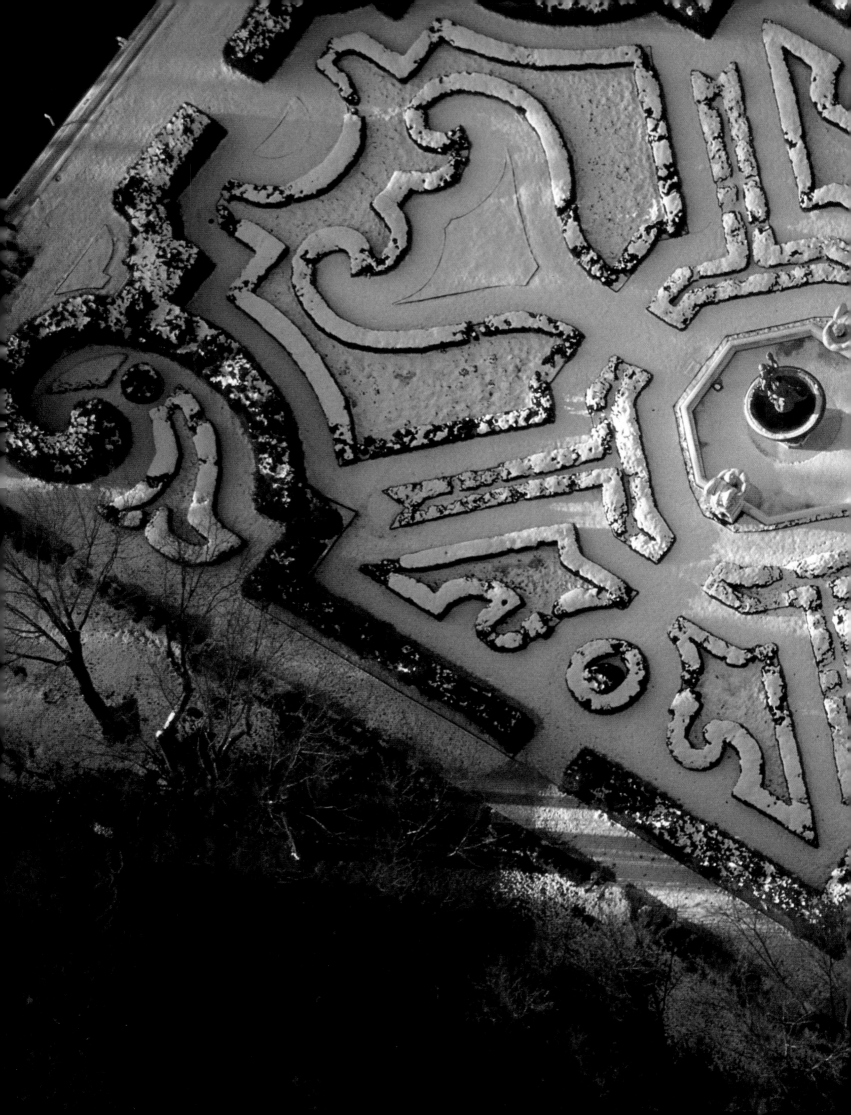

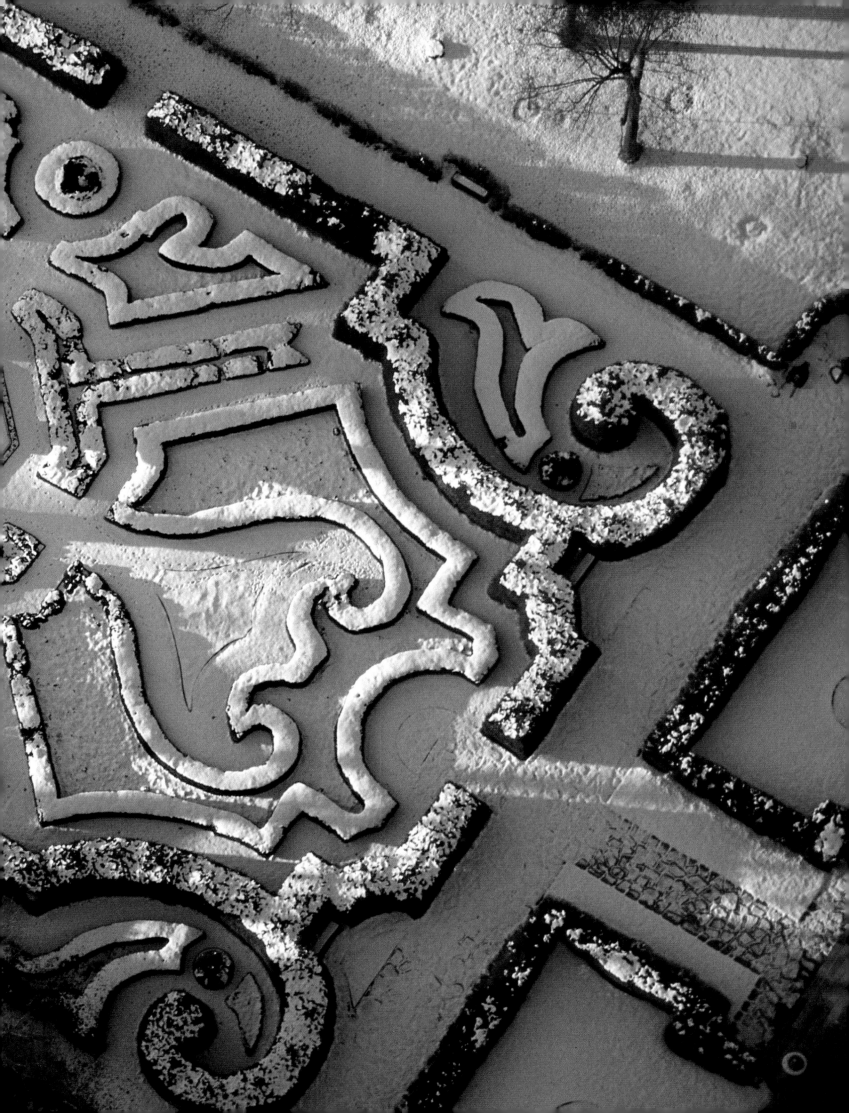

Agriculture consultant Stewart Ramsey Jr. chose fall's familiar face for his first corn maze (preceding pages). "I call it my Jack O'Lantern Maze. Cutting it in was difficult because we waited too long. The corn was too high," he says of the four-and-a-half-acre plot on Thompson's Bridge Road next to his popular Ramsey's Pumpkin Patch.

The Maze Garden at Nemours (preceding pages) complements an unparalleled vista at Alfred I. duPont's 300-acre country estate north of Wilmington. The maze, with hedges of Canadian hemlock and Hellert holly, is tilted for visibility from the 102-room mansion, a modified Louis XVI chateau of Brandywine granite quarried on site. Henri Crenier's 11-foot bronze statue, "Achievement," centers the plot. The grounds are among America's finest examples of French gardens. After the death of his wife, Jessie Ball duPont, in 1970, duPont's will stipulated his pink stucco residence be opened to the public. Nemours opens for reservation-only tours May through November. duPont also founded the Alfred I. duPont Hospital for Children, a world-renowned facility, built in 1940 on the property.

Common throughout the state, the majestic great blue heron (left) finds inviting habitat on Augustine Creek. The creek and its productive marshes provide feeding grounds for one of the nation's largest great blue heron nesting colonies.

Day's end filters through Wilmington, darkening the Delaware River to the east (following pages). The state's major urban center is home to a diverse population of about 73,000. Many still celebrate their ethnicity, a proud legacy from European forebears who settled the city.

Kent County

In Delaware's agrarian heartland, Kent County's small-town charm blends seamlessly with government and industry. Festivals, fairs and parades stitch a human face on the First State's middle county where farmers, legislators, professionals, artisans and watermen weave a colorful fabric from everyday endeavor.

Digging in her family's Felton area potato farm, Jennifer Black (right) gets in touch with roots sown by her grandfather, Francis Bergold, a Kent County transplant from Long Island 50 years ago. "The land was reasonable and it's good here to raise crops," says the patriarch of Byfield Farms, first established on Delaware patriot Caesar Rodney's lands near Kitts Hummock. Bergold markets 250 acres of all-purpose potatoes from Maine to Florida and also grows wheat, barley and field corn. "I help out whenever I'm home," says Black, a college junior. "I grew up with potatoes and love to live on a farm. You have open space and it's so peaceful."

"We say Jeremy's got that Opie look. And he can pick a pretty good quart of berries," Jennifer Hobbs says of her youngest son's finesse in the family's one-acre strawberry field near Viola (following pages). The short-season fruit ripens by Memorial Day and attracts hundreds to the Hobbs' U-pick operation. "They'll pick up to dusk or until the field gets picked out. It's something we've done on the side for about eight years. We enjoy seeing the same people every year. They like their strawberries."

A fifth-generation grain farmer and tavern owner, Bill Paskey relaxes with daughter Taylor Lynn (preceding pages) in the backyard he's named Deer Park, a 3-acre hamlet of vintage buildings, railroad siding and rolling stock. "The theme's like a time machine. Imagine yourself in an old farmhouse or one-room schoolhouse or country store. We even have an old captain's shack from Bowers Beach. The boxcar, caboose and old locomotive are filled too, mostly with train collectibles and pictures." Paskey welcomes the community to Deer Park for church picnics and school field trips. "I collect whenever I can get away," he says. "I've always been able to save up for my pastime. I'm never done collecting."

"It's an eye-catcher, not real little, not real big, but it's what people like best," incurable collector Paskey says of the rare 1940s Model S Case tractor wedged in his Felton farm museum (left) with thousands of antique toys, tools, trucks and other tractors. "There's so much stuff, it's just overwhelming. It's a private hobby just for show, never for sale. I keep bringing more stuff home from flea markets. People give me a lot too."

Divided by the Murderkill River, Bowers Beach and South Bowers (preceding pages) harbor much of Kent County's crab industry.

Rolling into another season, Dicky Moor (left) readies Leipsic crab boats for the catch in Delaware Bay and beyond. "Usually we're out by the first of May. All depends on the water temperature and if there's going to be any crabs. You get a real cold winter, a lot of ice, and that kills a lot of crabs," says the former eeler who baits 200 crab pots – the maximum allowed by Delaware law – with bunker or menhaden and sets them four miles out in the bay. "I got into full-time crabbing about 14 years ago. I've had one bad year, pretty good years and really good years."

Veteran waterman Jim Dare of Magnolia readies a collar for a catch of crabs (above). "You take the top half of a basket, turn it upside down and put it over the basket you're filling to make it overflow. You want a nice count before you put the lid on. The spring run is mainly sooks or females. Next will be peelers – crabs getting ready to shed – then the summer jimmy run, the blue-claw males. This area's always been real high-producing for crabs," says Dare, a Vietnam veteran whose great-great-grandfather built Saxton United Methodist Church in Bowers Beach.

At dawn, a crabber (following pages) churns east from Bowers Beach to check his pots.

"It's pretty much 'This Old House' except without Norm and his crew," Smyrna resident Scott Clark says of his mid-1800s Federal fixer-upper on Commerce Street (preceding pages). He and his wife, Sandra, bought the house in 1996. "We cleaned the dirt off the window and saw 10-foot ceilings, 12-inch plaster crown molding, two slate fireplaces and a humongous living room. We fell in love with it." Framed by raised panel plantation shutters, Clark pulls maintenance on windows too large to be original. "I'll be restoring this house for the next 20 years. You'll have to take the spackle knife out of my hand when I die."

Nearby, Cathy Cole catches a ride with friend Kristi Ayala as her twin Cassi looks on (left). "It's the only tire swing in the neighborhood," Cole says of the popular pendulum roped to a black oak tree in the sisters' front yard.

Pedal power cycles Dover police officers Gerald Perry and Chris White (above) closer to the city's 32,135 residents. "The bottom line," former Dover Police Chief Keith I. Faulkner says, "is bicycles put us in touch with the community and the community with us." Of the 81 law enforcement officers the Smyrna native commanded, five are assigned to the Dover Police Department's bike patrol. A federal grant bought the first bicycles in 1990.

Squatters' rights take a front seat near Marydel for Shari Wilbur, Joel Marousek and their sons, Critter, Little Hippie and Squirt (left). "Joel works as a custodian and brings toilets home all the time. We don't advertise but people drive by and see them," Shari says. "It took a little while for the first ones to sell but they've finally started going. They're only $20 and people buy them for remodeling and for personal use. We use the extra income for odds and ends."

"Nobody wants to do what I do 'cause it's too much trouble," says basketmaker Floyd Hrupsa (following pages) of Felton. "Takes me three to four hours on each basket, time I saw from the tree 'till I finish." Hrupsa, whose grandfather, Thomas Minner, operated a basket mill at Masten's Corner, fashions three sizes of baskets from red cedar or walnut using a form from Minner's mill. "See the Xs? That means they're handmade. Can't do that on a machine." Hrupsa demonstrates his dying art at Delaware, Maryland and Pennsylvania antique shows where his large baskets retail for $25. A retired state employee, Hrupsa stables a 1952 Dodge truck in a neighbor's lean-to. "Used it to haul grain when I was farming on the side. Don't want to get rid of it 'cause it's antique and still in good shape. Odometer's been 'round once so it's really got 152,000 miles."

Smyrna sculptor Richard H. Bailey (left) loses his abstract and realistic marbles to scores of satisfied customers who pay premium prices for a chip off his blocks. "People like marble. I have more than 100 varieties," he says. "I also work in granite, onyx, jade, jasper and semiprecious stones." Bailey exhibits his popular stone sculptures at numerous East Coast galleries, including New York City's Museum of Natural History. Shadowed by 3-ton marble columns from a Philadelphia library, he sands an original cross of white marble. The native Kent Countian prefers working outdoors and stores his tools in a converted pony barn on his mother's farm.

Dover folk artist Nina Spencer (above) is known for her tile and canvas paintings in primary colors. "All my art tells stories. I do a lot of spiritual and religious themes like baptisms in water and old country churches," says the self-taught Baptist preacher's daughter from Louisiana. "I also do some Old South, like cotton picking. My work is very simple and honest. Angels guide my hand and my paint just flows." Spencer credits her father for inspiring her career. "I talked too much so my daddy got me a little paint set, some overalls and set up an easel. That's how it's been ever since."

Framed by Delaware illustrator Frank Schoonover's works, curator Roxanne Stanulis (left) and director Karol Schmiegel usher impressionist Robert Reid's "A Summer Girl" to another gallery at the Sewell C. Biggs Museum of American Art in Dover. More than 500 objects are displayed on two floors above the Delaware State Visitor Center on Duke of York Street. Paintings, furniture and silver fill 14 galleries of the museum, which opened in 1993. "The museum is unique in that it is based on the collection of one man, Sewell C. Biggs," says Stanulis. "The focus is regional with a very good representation of objects by Delaware artists." The

Schoonover Gallery, she adds, is the only gallery in the Dover museum wholly devoted to one artist.

Assistant Bruce Decker (above) creates his own still life with 18th century objects in the museum's first gallery. The circa 1750 tall clock on the right contains works by George Crow, one of Wilmington's earliest clockmakers. Duncan Beard of Appoquinimink made the movement for the 1770s tall clock. Crafted in Delaware before 1765, the Queen Anne chairs descended through the Loockerman family of Dover. New Castle-born Anna Dorothea Finney chose blue for her circa 1760 portrait by John Hesselius.

Greatest show on First State turf, the Delaware State Fair amuses, thrills, entertains and educates crowds topping 200,000 during its 10-day run each July. Incorporated in 1919 as the non-profit Kent & Sussex County Fair, the agrarian-based event tempts all ages to the 90-acre fairgrounds in Harrington. "It's such a family event," says general manager Dennis Hazzard. "People still have an interest in letting their kids know where milk comes from."

Kelsey Grace of Smyrna (above) shows off Brady's Lady at the fair's Pretty Animal Contest. "I think we should have won," Kelsey said after losing to a mule.

Young farmers man a cow wash (following pages) at the fair where bovines milk a lot of attention. Dairy farming is a $25 million slice of Delaware's agricultural pie with about 95 dairy farms producing nearly 14 million gallons of milk annually.

Trainer John E. Veazey of Laurel warms up his Standardbred Niacrombie (right) on Harrington Raceway's half-mile stone dust track. "Our most important race," facilities director Karen Craft says, "is the $40,000 Governor's Cup during the Delaware State Fair." The track, established on the fairgrounds in 1946 as the Kent and Sussex Raceway, clocks 90 days of spring and fall racing. "Our purses average in excess of $100,000 a night. That's very favorable to the horsemen and gives them a chance to upgrade their stock and enhance harness racing."

Delaware's horseracing industry trotted past extinction in 1995 when the General Assembly passed the Horse Racing Preservation Act legalizing slot machines at Harrington Raceway, Dover Downs in Dover and Delaware Park in

Stanton. With slots revenues tallying $485 million in 2000, the tracks galloped to victory. And with about 92 percent returned on every dollar wagered, slots players smile too.

"The best part is winning, of course, and most all the time I come away a winner," Pat Prowell (above) says between bets at Dover Downs' Las Vegas-style casino.

Mustard on the side, trainer Karen Moore paces retired harness racer Displain (following pages) near Smyrna. "A cross country pleasure ride freshens him up so he doesn't get bored," she says of the 12-year-old Standardbred stallion, a lucrative Delaware Stakes Program sire.

In the pink, peach trees at Fifer Orchards west of Wyoming spring into production, yielding 72,000 baskets of 25 varieties of peaches during the 10-week season starting in late June. "It's really a wonderful heritage we have. There's something special about being linked to growing things," says Mary Fennemore, third-generation owner with her brother, Carlton Fifer (left). His oldest sons, David and Bobby, also work in the business established in 1919 by patriarch Charles Frederick Fifer Sr., a farmer from Virginia's Shenandoah Valley. Apples, sweet corn, peaches and asparagus headline the harvest from the family's 2,500-acre spread. Strawberries, cantaloupes, tomatoes, plums, potatoes, nectarines, broccoli, pears and pumpkins are also available in season. "People enjoy coming to a farm setting even if they can go to a grocery store and buy just about anything," Fennemore says. "But you can't beat the freshness here." Peaches vaulted Kent County to world prominence in 1869 with more than a million trees in production. Although a disease called "the yellows" later ended Delaware's reign as the Peach State, the General Assembly in 1895 adopted the peach blossom as the state flower. "We started a customer appreciation day back in the early 1980s and served peach ice cream cones," says Carlton. "In 1990, the town of Wyoming started the Peach Festival. We combined the two events and the festival's grown every year." Now Fifer Orchards scoops 10,000 free cones each August using more than 500 gallons of peach ice cream. "People around here like ice cream. I sure had my share that day."

Irish eyes smiling, Marissa Grinstead and Danielle Patterson (below) of Daisy Troop 1092 prepare to step off in the St. Patrick's Day Parade in Dover. "Everybody's Irish on St. Patrick's Day," says Lorraine Goodman, former director of Main Street Dover, sponsor of the 90-minute parade that lines Loockerman Street with a crowd of 7,000. "Not more than 20 of us, including Irish wolfhounds, marched the first year, 1994," recalls Mary Fitzpatrick, past president of the 80-member Irish Society of Delmarva. "Now, your adrenaline's going and there's a lot of camaraderie," adds the Dublin native who always dresses as a leprechaun and dances a jig. "The crowd really gets into it with clapping and singing."

Danielle Herrmann and Ashley Krueger (left) of Girl Scout

Troop 421 doff hats before marching in the 87-unit parade.

"Our claim to fame is maypole dancing on May Day. It's the single thing that makes us different," says Mary Skelton, chairman of Old Dover Days (following pages), a three-day festival celebrating Dover's Colonial heritage. "I never have to worry about attendance for the maypole dance because we have several area elementary schools participating and all the children's parents, grandparents, brothers and sisters show up." Complemented by Colonial crafts demonstrations, a juried Arts Festival and a parade, the event, inaugurated by Friends of Old Dover in 1933, draws 10,000 to The Green, Legislative Mall and other venues. "We're the city's largest and oldest festival and probably one of the oldest in the nation," Skelton says. "We've even been on Jeopardy!."

Called the "Cradle of Methodism," Barratt's Chapel (left) near Frederica begat the Methodist Episcopal Church in America. An inlaid brass star on the floor marks the meeting of Bishop Thomas Coke and clergyman Francis Asbury who formulated plans on November 14, 1784, for a church separate from the Anglicans' Protestant Episcopal Church. Coke for the first time administered sacraments in an American Methodist service. Land for the chapel in South Murderkill Hundred was conveyed in 1780 by Phillip Barratt, a converted Methodist farmer and Kent County sheriff. Built the same year, the nearly square Georgian structure stands as the nation's oldest house of worship constructed for and by a Methodist Society.

"Our family's not gotten 50 miles in 300 years," says Armstrong Barratt Cullen III (above) of Rehoboth Beach inside Barratt's Chapel with his father, Armstrong Barratt Cullen Jr. of Dover, and son Armstrong Barratt Cullen IV, 16, direct descendants of Phillip Barratt. Phillip's son, John Barratt, whose portrait hangs over the eldest Cullen's living room fireplace, was Delaware's secretary of state in 1810. His daughter was Mary Barratt Cullen. "It was kinda cool, how the building looked and the worn-down stones in the cemetery," the youngest Cullen says of his first visit to Barratt's Chapel. "I don't know many fourths. I have my full name on my State of Delaware boater's license but that's the only thing. If I have a son, I'd consider passing my name on. It's been passed on for hundreds of years. That's kinda cool."

On promised land, members of the Jireh Christian Center celebrate their first worship service. Eight days of rejoicing reverberated over the 42-acre site west of Dover, acquired in 1985 soon after the center was established. "We had 60 members, young families, and $50 in our church checking account then, but knew we wanted land to build on," says Pastor Miriam Mast. "People got excited about our vision and handed us $1,000 checks. We came up with a $40,000 down payment – I consider that a huge miracle – and we paid off the rest of the land." With a building fund of nearly $90,000, members built their new center. "We'd been meeting in the old theater at the Blue Hen Mall. People didn't want to go back," Mast says of the 200-member flock she ministers with ordained husband Dale. "Jireh is a Hebrew word that means 'the Lord who sees and provides.' We know people aren't happy-clappy. One of our goals is to see they get healing so they can become free to lead fruitful, productive lives."

Boyhood home of 18th century Delaware patriot John Dickinson, Poplar Hall on Jones Neck southeast of Dover (right) survives as a National Historic Landmark and state museum. A Tory looting of the Georgian mansion in 1781 prompted Dickinson, one of Kent County's largest land-owners, to accept the Delaware presidency after Caesar Rodney's term expired to bolster Delaware's militia during the Revolutionary period. Also president of Pennsylvania, he was among the last state presidents. Article 3 of the Delaware Constitution, ratified in 1792, changed the title to governor. Throughout his public life, Dickinson also maintained homes in Wilmington and Philadelphia. In 1804, a spark from the parlor chimney ignited Poplar Hall's cedar shake roof, burning the 1740 dwelling's wooden infrastructure,

leaving only the brick walls. An easterly wind contained the fire to the house's oldest section. Dickinson rebuilt the home two years later, redesigning the roofline as it appears today. Once more than 3,000 acres along the St. Jones River, Dickinson's plantation of cherry, plum, peach and apple orchards also produced wheat, corn and flax. Slaves and tenants farmed the land, inhabiting dirt floor dwellings (above) with enclosed plots for their root vegetables and herbs. Other outbuildings on the restored site that opened in 1956 include a granary, feed barn, stable, smokehouse and corncrib. "We're privileged having a lot of information on John Dickinson's plantation," says site supervisor Edward McWilliams. "That makes the museum, which is open year-round, very unique. We know what happened here."

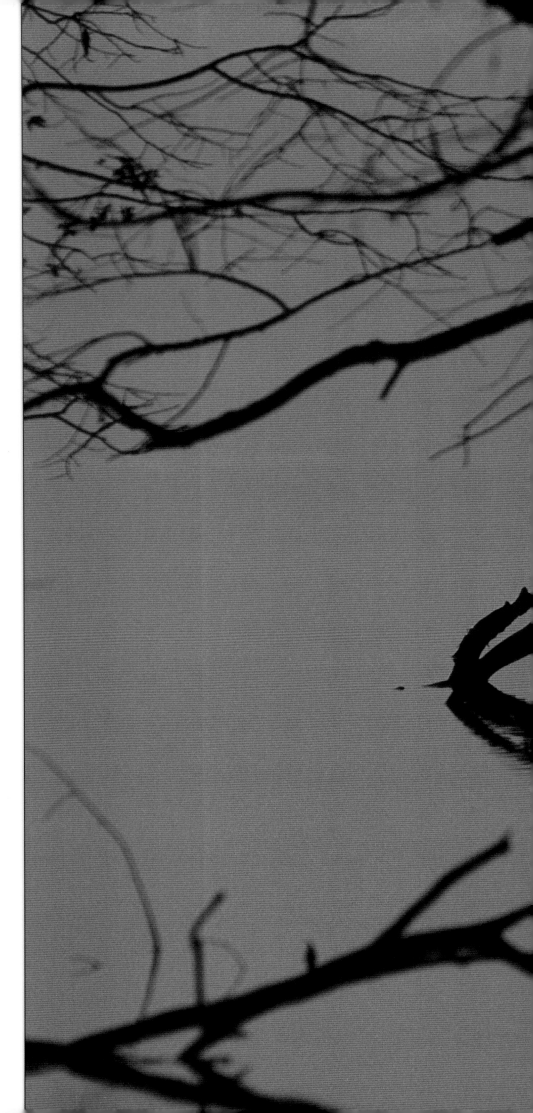

"We have national recognition as an important area for migrating birds," says Bombay Hook National Wildlife Refuge wildlife biologist Frank Smith. "It's a famous place for people who know a lot about waterfowl and shorebirds." Snow geese arrive in early October from Arctic Circle and northern Canada nesting grounds and their population peaks at 198,000 a month later. "They consume a lot of food while they're here and compete with Canada geese for corn and winter wheat, but they do some good things, like open areas of dense vegetation to allow other species to come in and feed."

Other refuge residents include the more solitary great blue heron (right). "We have maybe 100 and you'll see them in the water feeding on frogs, fish and small snakes," Smith says. "They're common throughout the state. Some will spend the entire winter here. If things freeze up, they'll move south." Bombay Hook offers safe haven to more than 100,000 migrating and wintering waterfowl. Established in northeastern Kent County in 1937, the refuge is one of more than 500 administered by the U.S. Fish and Wildlife Service. Tidal salt marsh, a valuable wildlife habitat, comprises three-quarters of the refuge's nearly 16,000 acres, plaited by rivers, creeks, branches, ditches and guts. Refuge management programs, designed to develop and protect desirable migratory waterfowl habitat, include raising crops on 1,100 acres for supplemental food. A visitor center, 12-mile auto tour route, observation towers and nature trails are open to the public year-round.

Meandering toward Delaware Bay, nearby Taylor's Gut (following pages) laces Woodland Beach Wildlife Area, supporting tidal flats, woods with habitat for the soapwort gentian, a rare, fall-blooming wildflower, and a pageant of wildlife. Dudley C. Lunt recorded the unspoiled area's majesty in his 1968 narrative, "Taylor's Gut."

Corn shocks stud a farm west of Dover (left) where horsepower is four-footed and Old Order Amish ways have prevailed since Jacob K. Miller moved to Kent County from California on February 8, 1915 and bought the first Amish farm 10 days later. Still a significant agricultural community, Amish families own at least 100 farms, down from about 300 farms 10 years ago, and cultivate about four thousand acres.

Encroaching development and escalating land prices force increasing numbers to flee the area, leaving Amish boys near Pearson's Corner (above) facing an uncertain future.

At the Procter & Gamble Dover Wipes Company, production technician Bob Baines (below) is dwarfed by a roll of the material used in the manufacture of Pampers Baby Fresh Wipes. "One of these rolls affords the opportunity for many, many thousands of diaper changes since our product is used by moms and dads to care for their babies' skin," says company spokeswoman Justine Maggio. "We have a three-part operation here. We make, we pack and we ship." More than 300 employees support the operation at the West North Street site. "We were part of Scott Paper Company from 1972 to 1995 when we were sold to Kimberly-Clark. In 1996, Procter & Gamble aquired the Dover Wipes Company," Maggio says. "It's an excellent place to work with a great group of people and outstanding

benefits. But it would have to be for me to drive 140 miles every day to work here."

Pushing the envelope, ILC Dover workers inspect the laminated polyester skin of a 125-foot-long airship manufactured at the Frederica facility (right). "We're pinholing for defects with a 500-watt light," says project engineer Tim Miller. "Crews inside and out look for pinholes, like stars in the sky. Every square inch of the balloon gets a light inspection." With a helium volume of 68,000 cubic feet, this airship is ILC's smallest, just half the length of its largest. "Blockbuster, Budweiser, Sanyo, MetLife – you see them at sporting events. They're ours," Miller says. "Airships are only about 10 percent of ILC's business. We're best known for our space suits." "But airships are very unique," adds production manager Stella Rexrode. "And interest is growing."

"We refer to it as the Royal Charter Document. It is the actual document whereby King Charles II in 1682 transferred to his brother James, Duke of York, most of what is today the state of Delaware," says Delaware Public Archives spokesman Russ McCabe (left). The now-finished rotunda entrance to the archives is an $18 million expansion of the 1938 Leon deValinger, Jr. Hall of Records in Dover. "It is certainly one of our two most valuable documents, along with the state's 1787 U.S. Constitution ratification document. And it's in beautiful condition." The Charter Document, the deed from the Duke of York to William Penn and two 10,000-year leases, also dated 1682, descended through the Penn family in America. The documents, which constitute the basis of all Delaware's

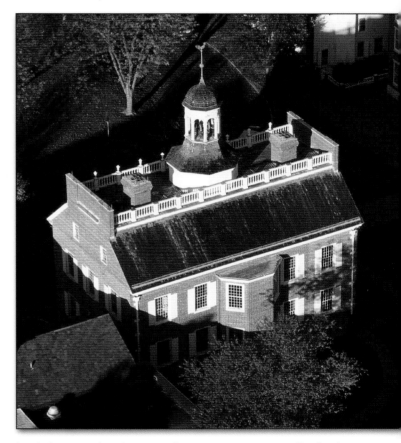

land claims and real estate titles, are on permanent display in the Hall of Records in Dover. "They are the state's chain of title and they belong to all citizens of Delaware," McCabe says. "The Charter is our crown jewel, from the king himself."

The State House on The Green in Dover (above) held its inaugural legislative session in May 1792, providing the General Assembly with its first permanent home since legislators vacated New Castle in 1777. Originally designed as the Kent County Court House, it was in continuous use as the state capitol until 1933 when lawmakers moved to their present quarters at Legislative Hall. One of eight state-owned museums, the State House was restored in 1976 for the Bicentennial.

Members of Delaware's 141st General Assembly convene in Legislative Hall in Dover. Delaware became the First State by being the first to ratify the U.S. Constitution on December 7, 1787. "Being a part of Delaware politics is extremely rewarding because you can make a difference," says five-term state Representative Nancy H. Wagner of Dover. "Because we're so small, we have to work together and no matter whom you talk to, everyone knows everyone."

Mighty wings, the C-5 Galaxy (following pages) is one of the largest aircraft in the world, capable of transporting Army combat equipment anywhere in the world at 518 miles per hour. Three dozen of the 247-foot-long behemoths are assigned to Dover Air Force Base, the only all C-5 wing in the U.S. Air Force. Operational in 1970, the Galaxy can be loaded and off-loaded simultaneously from nose and aft cargo openings and can take off and land in relatively short distances. The giant aircraft saw duty in Operation Desert Shield and Operation Desert Storm in the Persian Gulf and most recently in Yugoslavia. With aerial refueling, only crew endurance limits the length of the aircraft's journey.

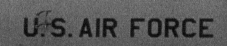

Downloading horsepower, NASCAR descends on Dover Downs International Speedway for Winston Cup racing in June and September. "People really get hooked on it," says Kent County sportswriter and author Gene Bryson. "It's fast, it's loud, the cars are colorful and it has a huge impact on the Dover area." The Delaware native has covered the sport for 22 years and recently wrote "Dover Downs NASCAR," a history of the mile-long track that opened in 1969. "Dover's a town of 31,000 and twice a year it grows to four or five times that," he says. "Hotel chains and restaurants race to open new accommodations before a race

weekend which generates about $40 million and brings 125,000 people into the area."

In the garage, NASCAR big wheels Jeff Gordon and Dale Jarrett (above) chat over carburetors. "They're friendly rivals. They're also among the top performers in the sport," Bryson says. "Both are class people and conduct themselves in that way. They have a lot of respect for each other." More corporate than ever, NASCAR racing is fueled by big money. "Corporate sponsorship drives the sport," Bryson says. "Huge companies spend about $10 million a year to put their names on cars (following pages). Look at the drivers. They're covered with sponsors' names too. It's all about money now."

THE HOME DEPOT
PONTIAC
GRAND PRIX
20
CLEVITE
MOOG
SIMPSON
76
WIX
26

"We were on fire," Caesar Rodney High School coach John Coveleski recalls after his Riders routed Tatnall School 11-5 for the state title (preceding pages). "It was a toss-up going into the game. Tatnall had more skill but we had a physical edge." Already a powerhouse, the Camden secondary school has won three State Boys Lacrosse Championships in the last decade. "Our program is only eight years old," says Coveleski, a veteran coach recruited from Delaware State University. "Lacrosse is the fastest growing sport in Delaware and our community chemistry is perfect for success. You need bright but hardened players with a passion for the game. We have a lot of bright, bright kids playing."

"I decided not to be mean and let her go ahead and spray me," Romanita Marshall of Milford (right) says of her cousin Danita LeGrand's prank. "I was washing my aunt's truck and

she came out to wash the hood. She got the hose and we started playing. It was cool. I was enjoying time with her."

Leaping off the Love Boat, Kimmie Burrows, cousin Faron Marshall and friends Asia Surguy, Katie Sipple, William Sipple and Jason Luff (above) plunge into the Leipsic River behind Sambo's, Kent County's landmark tavern and crab house lauded nationally for its jumbo lump crabcakes. "We try to give the best quality for the best price. We cook the old-fashioned way, over an open flame," says Elva Burrows, Sambo's owner with husband Isaac J. Burrows whose father, Samuel C. "Sambo" Burrows Sr., opened the Leipsic tavern and eatery in 1953. Isaac and Elva took over in 1985. "We're open April 1 through mid-November," Elva says. "And we're packed day and night."

"We wanted to create the best party ever in Dover," Frank Fantini (right) says of the Friends of the Capitol Theater's May benefit to preserve the 1904 Dover Opera House. "We're a theater so we can be theatrical. Each year we will re-create a classic movie. We started with 'The Great Gatsby' and re-created the 1920s on the shore of Silver Lake." As president of the Friends, Fantini leads the $7 million effort to expand and modernize the State Street landmark. The late Wilmington entrepreneur John W. Rollins Sr. and his wife, Michele, played major supporting roles in that effort with their $1 million donation. "When we're finished, in the fall of 2001, it will be a sister theater to

the Grand Opera House in Wilmington and will bring a new level of arts to Kent County. Our complex will be the Schwartz Center for the Arts in honor of the family who operated the building as the Capitol Theater from 1923 until it closed in 1982."

"My juniors work for six months to put on the Junior-Senior Prom," says Lake Forest art teacher and junior class advisor Lorrie McCartney. "It's the last real fun, let-it-all-hang-out activity before graduation and everyone loves to get dressed up." A bevy of beauties (above) cheers for Lake Forest's newly crowned Prom King and Queen. The coronation highlights an evening that includes an introductory grand march, dinner and dancing.

Delaware State University graduates (below) celebrate in Alumni Stadium after more than 400 received degrees at Delaware's historically black university. Founded by the 58th General Assembly in 1891 as the "State College for Colored Students," the university has evolved into a fully integrated, 400-acre campus north of Dover and culls a diverse student population from a dozen states and nine countries.

Deja McCoy hugs her friend Cashana Lewis (left) at the Dover African Festival. The Dover High School student is lead dancer for Sankofa African Drummers and Dancers and wears a *galae* or head wrap of two fabrics to match and accent her ceremonial dress. "I noticed a lack of artistic endeavor for minorities so I started the festival in 1991 to create a sense of cultural identity for African-Americans in central Delaware," recalls Dover City Councilman Reuben Salters, who visits

Africa annually. "I actually started it for the kids with the hope they would get enthused about their culture."

"There are no ghosts here, darn it," laments Jean Gruwell of Wheel of Fortune Farm (following pages), part of a William Penn land grant conveyed to John Chance in 1738. Gruwell and her husband, Hudson, a retired produce broker, bought the 250-acre farm near Leipsic in 1962. Punch and gouge molding and dog-eared door and window framing detail the circa 1750 Georgian manor house. Ax marks score the kitchen's original hand-hewn hemlock beams and brick milk and meat dependencies are still intact on the property bordering tidal Muddy Branch. The lone elm remains from a stand transported by ox cart in 1849 for planting on The Green in Dover. "The best part of living here," Gruwell says, "is the peace and quiet and the view. It's just gorgeous. We're blessed."

Bathed in the colors of dawn, Rehoboth Beach awakens to the new day's first footprints and yesterday's sandcastle masterpiece (left). The morning solitude soon will be washed away, replenished by summer throngs making tracks to claim the sandy playground. Anchored along Sussex County's 25-mile Atlantic coastline, First State beaches dominate as Delaware's most popular destination. Millions of visitors swell populations from Lewes to Fenwick Island, depositing more than $400 million into local resorts that bask in unprecedented prosperity.

Rehoboth Beach, nicknamed the "Nation's Summer Capital" for the seasonal influx of visitors from Washington, D.C., remains the flagship of family fun where crowds overflow the boardwalk and jam the beach (following pages) waiting for ocean-launched Independence Day fireworks.

Threading sea breezes with their 252-square foot parafoil, Rachel Hughes and Bee Linzey (following pages) stage an evening kite fly off Virginia Avenue in Rehoboth Beach.

Umbrellas provide an oceanside oasis near Henlopen Acres, an incorporated enclave of manicured homesites, a yacht basin and the Rehoboth Art League, the resort's cultural lifeline and site of the 1743 Homestead, the Rehoboth area's oldest house.
  Staking out his island in the sun, a young beach-goer (right) basks in summer pleasures at Sussex County's hottest seaside attraction.

Mastering broken waves at the East Coast Skimboarding Championships, an annual event in Dewey Beach since 1980, requires speed, agility, balance, lightning reaction and a boatload of daredevil tricks. Skimmer Bill Baxter sometimes sprints up to 50 yards on the beach before throwing his high-density foam boards on a broken wave – the skim – and riding it out to execute gravity-defying moves. An average ride lasts 10 seconds or less. "Beaches here are set up perfect. Dewey is world-famous for its shore breaks," says event founder Harry Wilson. "There's deep water right up to the beach and big waves dump hard."

151

Mile-square Rehoboth Beach (preceding pages) reigns as Delaware's premier resort famous for its beaches, tax-free shopping and fine dining.

The beach is a hot destination for Halie Murray-Davis (right) as she rolls into Rehoboth with a smile.

Volleyball spikes in popularity each summer in Rehoboth Beach. "It's probably one of our most important sports," says Tim Bamforth, the city's summer recreation director. "It's mostly pickup games, but there's diehard volleyball too." Tournaments decide the best players at the night courts off Baltimore Avenue where players tip off at 7 p.m. "The diehard guys are always on Court 1 which hosts the hot games of the night. There's usually a crowd on the boardwalk watching," Bamforth says. Wiffle ball, tether

ball and basketball also compete for free time at the beach playground across town from the city's day recreation area off Hickman Street. During spring and fall seasons, Mid-Atlantic Volleyball holds court with its First Rites of Summer and Mayor's Cup weekend tournaments that draw hundreds of amateurs to 70 nets stretched along a mile of beach.

Other athletes run with the Seashore Striders, a 15-year-old running club. About 5,000 participants lace up for the summer racing series at the beach. "The series is a huge event and attracts runners of all ages to Rehoboth," says Bamforth, also director of the nonprofit club.

Promoting cooperation and understanding within Rehoboth Beach's diverse population fulfills CAMP Rehoboth director Steve Elkins. "The acronym means 'Create A More Positive Rehoboth.' Primarily we promote the inclusion of gays and lesbians into the greater community," says Elkins, the openly gay co-founder of the non-profit organization with artist Murray Archibald, his partner of 23 years. "We're pioneers of a sort. Rehoboth's climate has changed dramatically and we've helped make a smoother transition by giving the city a forum to talk about change," he says. "We're not Key West and we're not Provincetown and we don't want to be. Most of us come to Rehoboth because we like the inclusiveness and the embracing quality. We feel we're helping the community live up to its biblical name, 'room for all.' Gays and lesbians are more comfortable being open here." Every Labor Day weekend, CAMP Rehoboth sponsors Sundance, a sold-out, two-day fund-raiser that nets more than $150,000 for AIDS programs and gay and lesbian concerns. CAMP Rehoboth also seeks common ground with area medical and religious sectors and works to ensure sensitivity by area law enforcement agencies in their handling of harassment issues. Elkins also publishes the 15-issue Letters From CAMP Rehoboth magazine. "I think Rehoboth is one of the best places to live," he says. "When you put a face on the individual segments of the community and humanize it, when you put some heart into it, you find our stories as citizens of this community are much more similar than different."

Artistic prodigy Abraxas sketches in Cape
Henlopen State Park near the World War II
watchtower he popularized in his oil
painting "Lookout." Famous at 23 for
"First Light," his Cape Henlopen Light-
house study, the Lewes artist commands
up to $30,000 for his landscapes and
portraits. "I enhance realism, painting
possibilities other people don't usually
see," he says. "I want to enlighten, to bring
beauty back into art."

158

Harper Cullen (left) of Rehoboth Beach yields to a sea gull's sunset craving for Grotto pizza on the boardwalk. Golden links in the resort's commercial food chain, Grotto devours 1,200 tons of cheddar cheese, 200 tons of flour and 45,000 gallons of pizza sauce annually at its 15 Delaware restaurants.

Always a good ride, family-owned Funland in Rehoboth Beach amuses vacationers daily from Mother's Day to the weekend after Labor Day. Operated since 1962 by four generations of Fasnachts and hundreds of "Funlanders" – a high school and college student work force – the busy one-acre boardwalk amusement park offers 18 rides like the Sea Dragon (above), 12 Skee Ball alleys, 100 video games and no set closing time.

Able to energize crowds with a single song, Love Seed Mama Jump (right) now rocks far from its home port of Dewey Beach. The national act, an opener for the Beach Boys, Matchbox 20 and Beck, plays Atlanta to Boston. "We're a high energy pop rock 'n' roll band," says dynamic lead singer Rick Arzt, who credits the group's decade-old chemistry to "mutual respect, our love for making music and the energy we create together." The sky's the limit for

him, guitarists Will Stack and Brian Gore, bass guitarist Pete Wiedmann, drummer Paul Voshell and percussionist David James. "We'd like," Arzt adds, "to be rock stars on a global basis."

Visiting more than 30 local venues, thousands fall for the music at the Rehoboth Beach Autumn Jazz Festival, an October high note since 1989. Jazz legend Maynard Ferguson (above) blows his own horn outside the loop at a Midway steakhouse.

Hot wheels drive 130,000 spectators to the U.S. 13 Dragway and Delaware International Speedway north of Delmar each year. The family-owned 132-acre motor sports complex takes second place behind the beaches as Sussex County's top attraction. The National Hot Rod Association's southernmost Division I track, the quarter-mile dragway

hosts NHRA regional finals. March to October purses for weekly elapsed time races total about $200,000. Racing four stock car divisions on its half-mile clay oval from April to November, the speedway pays more than $400,000 in winnings every year. Drag racing draws more participants, stock cars more spectators.

179

Regional inhabitants for more than 10,000 years, Native Americans survive today in Delaware as Nanticokes, "people of the tidal waters," in the Riverdale area near Millsboro. "We're an endangered species with a long, proud history," says assistant chief Charles C. "Little Owl" Clark IV, an artist and writer. "There are only about 1,000 of us and about 75 percent live in lower Delaware." The Nanticokes celebrate their heritage with a September powwow that brings together 60 other tribes from across the nation and Canada. Dancing, drumming and storytelling sated with succotash, fry bread and Indian tacos highlight the two-day event revived in 1977. "The powwow went into a lull in the 1940s. Many men joined the service – the modern way of becoming a warrior – in World War II," Clark says. "The civil rights movement opened doors for Native Americans. After assimilation, it was OK to be an Indian. We looked for ways to re-establish and coalesce various aspects of our culture into one event." Powwows maintain the Nanticoke Indian Museum's trove of authentic arrowheads, stone tools, pottery and extensive Native American library. Thousands attend the Nanticoke Powwow, one of the East Coast's largest and recipient of the Governor's Tourism Award. "We try to educate people and want them to leave with a better understanding of native culture," Clark says. "We live and die, bleed and cry like everyone else."

Roots run deep for lifelong farmers Brad Hickman (above) of Selbyville and Delmus Hickman of Ocean View who are unrelated but share a love of their agrarian heritage. On Sundays, Brad airs his family's restored 1927 Chevrolet one-ton pickup that hauled chickens, ducks and guineas to Philadelphia during the Depression.

Delmus harvests truck crops in front of his 1947 corncrib. "I got a real mom-and-pop operation," he says. "I put my vegetables on a picnic bench under an umbrella in front of my house. That's my store."

"The more you eat, the more you want," promises Clara Williams, "Berry Boss" at Ryan's Berry Farm & Orchard, a 138-acre spread of reclaimed swampland near Frankford. Delaware's largest blueberry grower, Ryan's annually yields 200,000 pounds of the potassium-rich fruit. More than 50,000 customers pick 16 varieties of blueberries seven days a week from mid-June through July. "I keep 'em happy by telling 'em where the best berries are, yes indeedy," says Williams, culling experience from more than 50 summers in the patch she helped plant. "Clara's infamous," owner Tom Ryan says. "People come all the way from New York just to see her." Despite Clara's charismatic draw, 78 million pounds of watermelons a year far outweigh blueberries as Delaware's top fruit crop, followed by apples, cantaloupes, peaches and strawberries.

Golden smile, Dogfish Head Craft Brewery president Sam Calagione lofts a legend near Lewes at Delaware's only microbrewery. Uncorking his revolutionary Midas Touch on the Today Show prompted host Matt Lauer to gush over the golden elixir, part beer, part wine and part mead. Drunk at King Midas' funerary feast 2,700 years ago, the re-created regal brew sells nationally, joining Dogfish Head's best seller Shelter Pale Ale and its other Sussex County-bred beers. "We use no corn, rice or extracts in our non-pasteurized products," says Calagione. "We do use higher quality ingredients like 100 percent Delaware-grown barley and the difference, we believe, is in the taste of the beer."

With 10 acres of her family's alfalfa farm near Lewes under vine, a disarming but determined Peggy Raley (following pages) convinced the Delaware General Assembly in 1991 to pass legislation to allow wineries in the state. Two years later, she opened Nassau Valley Vineyards and remains proprietor of Delaware's only winery. "I love wine. It's part of the history of civilization," she says of the gift of the grape. Raley produces 3,000 cases of eight varieties of wine annually. Her Meadow's Edge White, Cape Rosé, Cabernet Sauvignon and Laurel's Red are favorites. "If the product I put on your table allows you to break bread and toast the lives around you and let go of all your daily worries, then I've done my job."

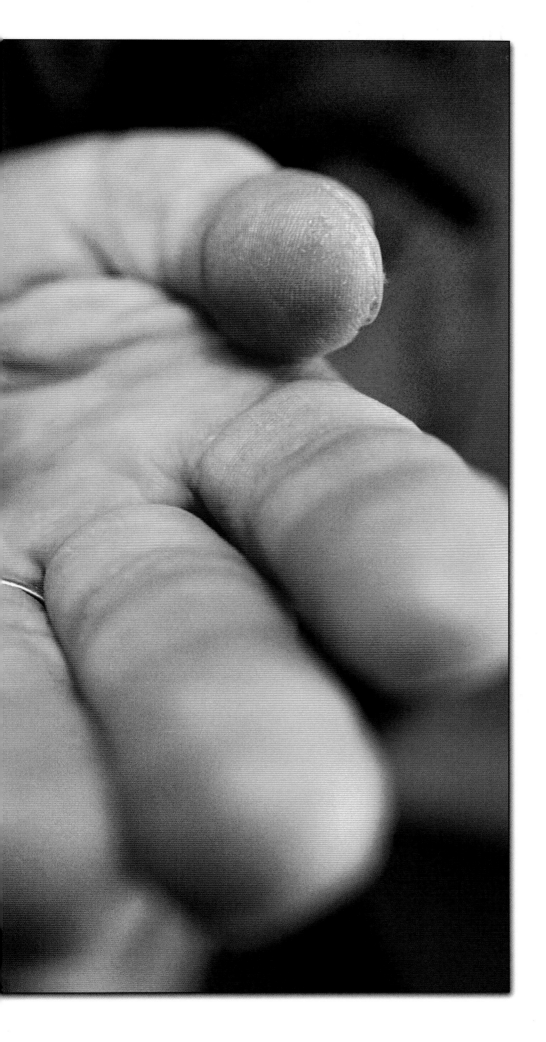

Come fall, tenant Brenda Johnson stores black walnuts in Paul Pepper's 1942 broiler house near Selbyville (preceding pages). "No one wants to crack walnuts anymore," laments Pepper. "I'll put 'em in there for the squirrels. We used to dry 'em til they were crispy, run 'em through a corn sheller then tap 'em with a hammer. Now people buy 'em in a package."

Chickens rule the roost in Sussex County, one of the nation's biggest poultry-producing counties. Nearly 700 contract growers produce about 250 million birds annually – three percent of the country's total broiler production – for Mountaire, Allen's Family Foods, Perdue Farms and Tyson Foods. Hours after hatching, baby chicks board a bus to a contract grower's poultry house. In the next 45 to 52 days, each bird eats two pounds of feed for every pound it weighs. "Chicken is the most efficient animal to convert grain protein into meat protein," says Charles C. "Chick" Allen III, president of Seaford-based Allen's Family Foods.

"I herd 'em up and run 'em into a pen. Then we catch seven, sometimes five or six, at a time by one leg," says professional chicken catcher Richard Parker (following pages) as he works a Mountaire poultry house near Millsboro. The gang of six catchers will cage the house's entire population of 21,000 birds in three to four hours and move on to the next house.

No one remembers when chicken first came off the grill at the Greenwood barbecue (following pages). But everyone knows the Greenwood Volunteer Fire Company and the Greenwood VFW do chicken right. Patrons pile into a pole-shed flanked by picnic tables on the U.S. 13 median to purchase 2,500 platters every summer weekend. "I eat a whole lot more smoke cooking chicken than I do fighting a fire," says David Haymond as he and David Warner baste chicken halves with a special sauce. Ingredients are a closely guarded secret.

A curious concoction of pig snouts, jowls, tongues, livers, hearts, cornmeal, flour and special seasonings, scrapple is Sussex County's signature side dish. RAPA Scrapple in Bridgeville is the largest of Delaware's four purveyors and processes up to 48,000 pounds daily for markets in five states and Washington, D.C. Varieties of RAPA's one- and two-pound scrapple bricks include "Our Original," "Hot & Spicy," "With Bacon" and beef scrapple. Of Pennsylvania Dutch origin, the breakfast staple is sliced, fried and often finished with ketchup, mustard or maple syrup. Founded in 1926 by brothers Ralph and Paul Adams, RAPA was sold in 1981 to a Wisconsin company. Ernest Lofland (left), one of 44 employees, stirs a 1,000-pound-capacity stainless steel pot in the company's cavernous kitchen. Each October, RAPA celebrates its culinary coup by co-sponsoring the Apple Scrapple Festival with local orchard owners T.S. Smith & Sons. Highlight is the scrapple carving contest. "There are two things you don't want to know about Delaware," quips one local. "What goes into politics and what goes into scrapple."

Competitive pumpkin hurling attracts international media attention and plants 15,000 spectators in a Sussex County soybean field. "Where else can you see pumpkins fly?" asks Carol Ostasewski (left), secretary of the 300-member Punkin Chunkin Association. Dubbed "Delaware's home-grown insanity," the World Championship Punkin Chunk germinated in 1985 after a Lewes blacksmith, a Harbeson plumber and a Georgetown well driller got their gourds together. Today, teams chunk for best distance – and charity.

Little Miss Millsboro hopefuls (preceding pages) contend with nervous butterflies before judging begins. Pageants, from Little Miss Fire Prevention to Dairy Princess to Watermelon Queen, make up much of Sussex County's social fabric and prep contestants for the Miss Delaware Scholarship Pageant, the state's most coveted crown.

History reigns over Georgetown on Return Day, a biennial balm for healing political wounds, when winners and losers parade together two days after November elections. Voters' first opportunity more than 200 years ago to hear poll results in the county seat, the uniquely Delaware event – now a mandated half-day holiday in Sussex County – survives as a festive forum for political reconciliation. Party leaders symbolically bury the hatchet and crowds averaging 30,000 feed on free ox sandwiches. Return Day crier Layton Johnson (right), Georgetown's longest-serving mayor, prepares to read the results from the Sussex County Courthouse balcony overlooking The Circle.

Officiating at a baptism, Pastor Charles Holland immerses one of his New Hope Assembly Church members in the still waters of Trap Pond near Laurel. "They separate from their sinful life," Holland explains. "When they come to the baptism and say they accept Christ in their lives that excites me and makes me feel spiritually elevated."

No cross too heavy, retired Episcopal minister Dick Swartout frequents Old Christ Church near Laurel, built in 1771-1772 as a "chapel of ease" or branch church of Stepney Parish, Maryland. The rare, unaltered pre-Revolutionary building remains without electricity, heat or plumbing. Its two-tiered pulpit, 43 box pews and east wall chancel – all of heart pine – are architecturally unparalleled. Maintained and administered since 1922 by the Old Christ Church League, the building is owned by St. Philip's Episcopal Church in Laurel and is open Sunday afternoons from April to October and July 4. "There's a special feeling you get when you walk in that says this is a holy place," Swartout says. "Think of how many prayers have been prayed here."

Suspended in seasonal limbo, an early frost clings to maple leaves near Georgetown.

Sunset washes over fall foliage (preceding pages), shadowing farmland east of Milford where earth tones contrast with a monochromatic creek meandering toward the Delaware Bay.

An ethereal Trussum Pond (following pages), home of one of the northernmost stands of bald cypress trees, waits out winter within Trap Pond State Park in southwestern Sussex County.

Second reapers of corn and soybean fields, snow geese (following pages) fly from Prime Hook National Wildlife Refuge near Broadkill Beach in search of grains and grasses. Rare in Delaware before the 1970s, now nearly 300,000 migrate each fall from Canadian breeding grounds, often destroying valuable crops and fragile wetlands in their wake.

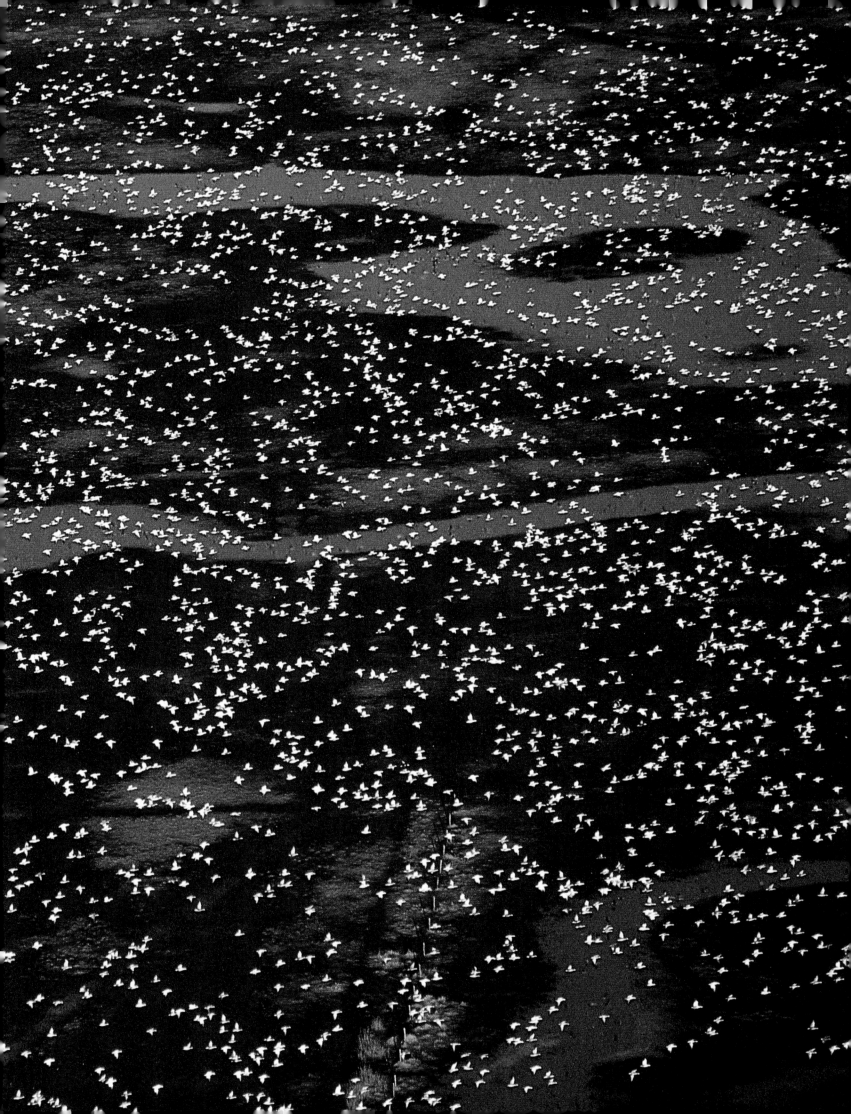

Quail Jones (left) unwinds outside Signs of the Past, a converted 1930s poultry feedhouse near Georgetown where he sells antiques, glass, collectibles and his specialty, old advertising signs. "Condition's a great part of their value," he says of his 300-plus collection of mostly metal signs, rated good to "near mint" and tagged $20 to $2,000. "Old signs have nice graphics and brilliant colors. They're works of art. The excitement is finding something I've never seen."

Frankford innkeeper Ray Davis (following pages) relaxes with his retriever Nikki on the wraparound veranda of the 1870s Captain Ebe T. Chandler House. "A lot of our guests like the beach but not the crowds," he says, "We're close enough so they can spend the day at the beach yet come back here to peace and quiet. Frankford's a nice small town."

No remedy for the faint of heart, Milton family practitioner and master balloonist Dr. Charles Wagner (following pages) prescribes sunrise ballooning over Indian River Bay.

Twilight travelers navigate shifting sands near the fabled World
War II submarine watch towers in Cape Henlopen State Park.

Portfolio Books
Post Office Box 156 • Rehoboth Beach, Delaware 19971
800-291-7600

proofreading by Ken Mammarella and J.L. Miller
history consultant Hazel D. Brittingham

printed and bound in Hong Kong by Dai Nippon Printing Company, Ltd.

The East End Light on the breakwater in Lewes (endsheet) guided
mariners from 1885 until its 1996 decommission by the U.S. Coast Guard.